Contents

20

33

43

From the Staff

Whether you're a seasoned machine quilter or a novice who's always wanted to learn to machine-quilt, this one-stop, quilter-tested reference guide will show you everything you need to know about this exciting technique.

In *Teach Yourself to Machine-Quilt* we've included information about all the basic supplies you'll need, plus an assortment of useful gadgets you might enjoy adding to your quilting cache (pages 2–17). You'll also find step-by-step how-tos, a gallery of inspiring quilting patterns to peruse (pages 29–34), and loads of useful tips and ideas scattered throughout—all aimed at making quilting easier for you and more fun. And to showcase your refreshed or newly acquired machine-quilting skills, choose one or all three of the featured quilts (pages 35–48).

We hope you'll enjoy this guide, that you'll refer to it often over the years, and that it helps make your machine quilting even more satisfying.

Happy Quilting!

A Look at the Supplies

QUILTING SUPPLIES CAN BE AS basic as scissors, needle, and thread or more complex with specialty tools designed for a specific purpose. There are hundreds of items available to make quilting tasks easier, more accurate, and more fun. Whether you're a gadget lover or a minimalist, knowing what the tools are, what to use them for, and why they're useful is essential.

Marking Tools

Many products are available for marking sewing lines and quilting designs on a quilt top. Useful supplies include fabric markers, templates, and pattern guides.

Variances in fabric contrast (light to dark) and fabric quality make marking different for each project. A variety of markers may be needed for a single project. Before you begin to mark your quilt top, try markers on fabric scraps and wash the test scraps as you will the quilt to be sure the marks will wash out.

Templates and pattern guides will vary according to the needs of each project.

FABRIC MARKERS

Artist's pencil: This silver pencil often works on both light and dark fabrics.

Chalk pencil: The chalk tends to brush away, so it is best to mark as you go with this pencil.

Mechanical pencil: Use hard lead (0.5) and mark lightly so that stitching or quilting will cover it.

Pounce: This is chalk in a bag. Pounce or pat the bag on a stencil, leaving a chalk design on the fabric. The chalk disappears easily, so mark as you go with a pounce.

Soap sliver: Sharpen the edges of leftover soap for a marker that washes out easily.

Soapstone marker: If kept sharp, this marker will show up on light and dark fabrics.

Wash-out graphite marker: Keep the sharpener handy for this marker that works well on both light and dark fabrics.

Wash-out pen or pencil: Either of these markers maintains a point and is easy to see. Refer to the manufacturer's instructions to remove the markings and test them on fabric scraps to make sure the marks will wash out. *Note: Humidity may make the marks disappear, and applying heat to them may make them permanent.*

TEMPLATES AND PATTERN GUIDES

A template is a pattern made from extra-sturdy material so you can trace around it many times without wearing away the edges.

Quilting stencils and templates: Precut stencils and templates in a variety of shapes and sizes, *above,* are available from quilt shops. These may be made from template plastic or a heavier-weight acrylic plastic. They can be traced around multiple times without wearing away any edges.

Some quilting stencils also are made from paper. They are designed to be stitched through and torn away after the design is completed.

TIP
When using any marking tool, keep the point sharp to get a fine, yet visible line.

Template plastic: Template plastic, *above,* is an easy-to-cut translucent material available at quilt shops and crafts supply stores. Its translucency allows you to trace a pattern directly onto its surface with permanent marker or pencil to make a stencil or template.

Test a variety of materials; some are heat-resistant (helpful when ironing over template

Selecting Scissors

edges), and some are not. Some varieties are gridded for accuracy in tracing or shaded for better visibility.

Freezer paper: Available at quilt shops and supermarkets, freezer paper allows you to create an iron-on template. You can trace a shape onto the dull side of the freezer paper, cut it out, and press it directly onto fabric with an iron.

Graph paper: You can use the printed lines on graph paper to draw a pattern piece. Glue the graph-paper pattern to template plastic, tag board, or cardboard. Allow the adhesive to dry before cutting through all layers at once to make an accurate template.

Clear vinyl: Also known as upholstery vinyl, this material is used by hand quilters to make overlays for accurately positioning appliqué pieces on foundation fabric.

Tape: Several types of tape are used to mark quilting and stitching lines; quilter's tape, painter's tape, paper tape, and masking tape are common choices. Quilter's tape is exactly ¼" wide; place it at the edge of your fabric, and stitch alongside it for a ¼" seam allowance.

Specialty tapes in widths from ¹⁄₁₆" to 1" and wider are preprinted with lines to aid quilters in evenly spacing hand quilting or decorative stitches, such as a blanket stitch.

Some quilters use masking tape as a guide for straight-line machine or hand quilting. *Note: Do not leave masking tape on fabric for an extended period of time since the adhesive from the tape may leave a residue. Painter's tape is less sticky than masking tape and also can be used as a guide for straight-line quilting.*

Quilting requires a good pair of scissors. Most quilters use several pairs, each designed for a different purpose. Choose your cutting tools with care, making certain they are of the highest quality you can afford. It's better to have two or three sharp pairs of scissors than a drawer full of seldom-used, dull pairs.

Choose your scissors and shears from the following.

Thread clippers (A): Use for cutting threads. A single style is used by both left- and right-handed persons.

Craft scissors and knife-edge straight trimmers (B): Left- and right-handed styles are available.

Embroidery scissors (C): Use for thread cutting. Left- and right-handed styles are available.

Appliqué scissors (D): Use for close trimming; a special duckbill protects the underneath layers of fabric. Left- and right-handed styles are available.

Knife-edge bent trimmers or shears (E): Use for general cutting and sewing. The bent handle and flat edge provide accuracy when cutting on a flat surface. Left- and right-handed styles are available.

Spring-action scissors (F): Available in both small and large sizes, this style is ideal for use by persons with weakened hands or for lengthy cutting sessions. The scissors can be used by both left- and right-handed persons.

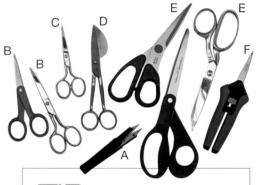

TIP In a pinch with no scissors in sight? Use nail clippers to cut your thread.

Can't see the lines of your ruler on the fabric? When working with dark fabrics, choose a ruler with yellow or white markings. For light fabrics, choose one with black markings.

Thread & Needles

Thread and needles are at the heart of quilting as the two elements that literally hold everything together. Choosing the right type and size needle and thread can make a big difference in the success of your quilting project. Follow three general guidelines: Match the thread type to the fabric fiber content, select the needle type based on the fabric being used, and select the needle size to match the thread.

THREAD

Thread has multiple roles, from holding together patchwork to anchoring the fabric to the batting. Thread also plays a role in decoration, adding color, design, and texture to the quilt surface.

For piecing and most quilting, it's best to match the thread fiber to the fabric. Since most quilters use cotton fabric, 100% cotton thread is the best thread choice. Cotton thread is equal in strength to cotton fabric and should wear evenly.

Synthetic threads, such as polyester, rayon, and nylon, are quite strong and can wear cotton fibers at the seams. For decorative quilting or embellishing, threads other than cotton may be appropriate.

Be sure your thread choice is suitable for the task; thread made for hand quilting, such as glazed cotton thread, should not be used in your sewing machine.

Thread Types

100% COTTON

Cotton thread is a staple in quilting. This thread works well with cotton fabric and is strong enough to create pieces that are durable. Hundreds of color choices are available in a variety of weights, although not all weights are created equal. Most cotton threads are two- or three-ply.

COTTON-WRAPPED POLYESTER

Wrapping cotton around a polyester core creates a stronger thread with the finish characteristics of cotton thread. This thread

TIP The fabric strength should be greater than that of the thread used for piecing. If seams are stressed, thread will give way before the fabric tears. For this reason, strong polyester thread should not be used for piecing cotton fabrics.

is best used with fabric blends because it provides a little stretch. It's important to use a needle with a large eye to prevent stripping the cotton wrap from the polyester core.

BOBBIN-FILL OR LINGERIE

Made from polyester or nylon and available in black or white, bobbin-fill works for machine embroidery, machine appliqué, or other decorative thread projects where multiple colors might be used in the needle. Prepare several bobbins filled with this thread so you can sew continuously without stopping to refill a bobbin.

This thread is lighter weight than 100% cotton thread, which will cause the top thread to pull slightly through to the back side of the piece. Bobbin-fill is a more economical alternative to filling bobbins with specialty threads.

METALLIC

The sheen and variety of colors available make metallic threads appealing for decorative stitching. However, metallic threads have a tendency to fray and break more often than cotton thread.

Using the right equipment will make the sewing process smoother. Work with a metallic or large-eye needle and a lightweight polyester, rayon, or nylon thread in the bobbin.

Depending on your sewing machine manufacturer's specifications, you also may add liquid silicone drops to the spool to make the thread run through the machine more easily.

Typical thread weights are 30, 40, 50, 60, and 80. If the number of plies is equal, the higher number indicates finer thread. For example, a 50-weight three-ply thread is finer than a 40-weight three-ply thread.

MONOFILAMENT

Available in clear or smoke color, this synthetic, lightweight thread comes in nylon and polyester. It generally is used for machine quilting when you don't want the quilting thread to show or where thread color may be an issue (e.g., quilting on multicolor prints). In the bobbin, use a lightweight cotton thread or bobbin-fill in a color that matches the backing.

POLYESTER

This thread is designed for sewing with knits because the filament has the same stretch as knit fabric. Polyester thread should not be used with cotton fabrics for piecing or quilting because it can be abrasive to soft cotton fibers and cause the fabric to tear at the seams.

RAYON

The soft, lustrous characteristics of rayon thread and the hundreds of colors available make it ideal for embellishment. It's often used for decorative quilting or embroidery. This thread is not strong enough and doesn't wear well enough to be used in piecing a quilt and should be alternated with a cotton thread when quilting a project that will get lots of wear.

SILK

Silk thread is stronger than cotton because it is a continuous filament, unlike cotton's short, spun fibers. Silk also has more stretch than cotton thread. Some quilters prefer to use silk

CHOOSING A THREAD COLOR

Match thread and fabric colors when you want the quilting design to blend in with the quilt top or backing, such as when stippling or quilting in the ditch. When you want to accentuate the quilting, choose a thread color in contrast to the fabric color. This may be especially important when using decorative threads as a strong design element.

thread for hand appliqué because it glides through the fabric more easily than cotton and is usually finer, thus making it easier to hide the stitches. It also is less prone to fraying, allowing a longer length of thread to be used.

VARIEGATED

This term applies to thread in which the color changes back and forth from light to dark throughout the strand or revolves through a range of colors to create a rainbow effect. It is available in both cotton and rayon.

WATER-SOLUBLE

This thread dissolves in water. Use it to baste a quilt or anchor trapunto or reverse appliqué. Once the project is completed, immerse it in water to dissolve the thread. Be sure to store the thread in a dry, humidity-controlled location.

> TIP Thread marked 50/3 (50 weight and 3 ply) works for both hand and machine quilting on cotton fabric. It's considered a medium-weight thread.

Troubleshooting Checklist for Thread Breakage

If you're having trouble with thread breaking, check these possible causes.

● **Damaged or incorrect needle:** Change the needle as it may be dull from overuse or have a burr or nick. If the needle is new, make sure it is the correct size and the eye is large enough for the thread type and weight being used (see chart, *opposite*).

● **Defective or old thread:** Lower-quality threads may have thick and thin spots that lead to breakage. Thread that is too old becomes brittle as it ages, causing it to break easily.

● **Improperly threaded machine:** Check to see that your spool is properly positioned on the sewing machine. The thread may be getting caught on the spool cap end as it comes off the top of the spool. The solution may be as simple as turning over the spool on the spool pin. Or if the presser foot wasn't raised when you threaded the machine, the thread may not be caught between the tension discs inside the machine. Simply remove the spool and rethread your machine with the presser foot raised.

● **Operator error:** Pushing or pulling on the fabric or allowing drag to be created by hanging a heavy quilt over your work surface can increase stress on the thread and cause breakage.

● **Tension too tight:** Refer to your machine's manual and page 15 to determine if this is the cause of your thread breakage.

● **Wrong thread:** You may have the wrong thread for your fabric. Change thread and sew on a fabric scrap to see how a different thread performs.

NEEDLES

Whether you sew by hand or machine, using the correct needle size and type will make the task easier and the results more polished.

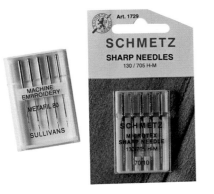

Machine- and hand-sewing needles have some similarities, but be aware that once you've mastered the numbers for machine-needle sizes, you'll need to learn a whole new set for hand-sewing needles.

It is important to change needles frequently as both kinds become dull with use. If a machine needle strikes a pin or the machine bed, it can develop a nick or burr that can tear your fabric.

The notions wall in your local quilt shop or sewing center can be intimidating if you're not sure what you need. There are dozens of sizes and shapes of sewing-machine needles,

> For machine needles, the larger the number, the larger the needle.

each designed for a different task. Understanding the terminology associated with machine needles can take the mystery out of making your selection and make your piecing and quilting go smoother.

Machine-Needle Sizes

When looking at a package of machine needles, you will often see two numbers separated by a slash mark. The number on the left of the slash is the European size (range of 60 to 120); the right-hand number is the American size (range of 8 to 21). Sizes 70/10, 80/12, and 90/14 are most commonly used for quilting. A lower number indicates a finer machine needle.

Machine-Needle Points

The needle point differentiates the type and purpose of a needle and is a key characteristic to consider when selecting a needle for a project. The needle point should match the fabric type. For sewing on quilting cotton, for example, use a needle labeled as a "sharp."

Anatomy of a Machine Needle

Shank: the part of the needle that goes into the machine.

Shaft: the body of the needle that extends below the shank.

Front Groove: the indentation on the front of the needle that allows the thread to lie close to the needle as it runs toward the bobbin. A deeper front groove can protect heavier thread from excess friction.

Scarf: the indentation on the back of the needle where the stitch is formed. When the bobbin shuttle swings into the scarf, it hooks into the looped thread on the needle to form the stitch.

Point: the tip of the needle. Select the point size based on the fabric being sewn.

Eye: the hole the thread passes through. Select the eye size based on thread type and weight.

THREAD AND COORDINATING MACHINE-NEEDLE SIZES

	60/8	70/10	75/11	80/12	90/14
Piecing and binding cotton fabric with cotton thread			●	●	
Piecing flannel					●
Quilting with monofilament thread	●	●	●	●	
Machine appliqué	●	●	●	●	
Sewing batiks, silks, or high thread-count fabrics with cotton thread		●			
Embellishing with decorative threads				●	●
Adding binding and borders			●	●	

Needles last longer when the fabric and batting used are 100% cotton. Polyester or polyester/cotton blend batting tends to dull needles quicker.

Machine-Needle Eyes

A needle's eye must be large enough for the thread to pass through with minimal friction. If the eye is too large for the thread, it may produce a seam that is loose and weak. Large needles make large holes, so use the smallest needle appropriate for the thread. Some needles have eyes specially shaped for certain thread types, such as metallic threads, to minimize breakage (see the Thread and Coordinating Machine-Needle Sizes chart on *page 7*).

Machine-Needle Types

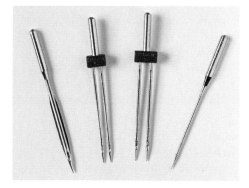

SHARPS are the preferred needle type for piecing and quilting woven fabrics such as cotton. Sharp needles come in a variety of sizes and brands.

UNIVERSAL NEEDLES can be used on both woven and knit fabrics but are not ideal for piecing because the needle points are slightly rounded. Choose this needle type if you want versatility when working with different fabrics.

METALLIC NEEDLES are designed for use with metallic threads. A larger needle eye accommodates the thread, which tends to be fragile yet rough enough to create burrs in the eye of the needle. Burrs can cause the thread to fray and break.

TOPSTITCH NEEDLES can handle heavier decorative threads but also leave larger holes in the fabric.

SPECIALTY NEEDLES include double or triple needles, leather needles, and heirloom-sewing needles.

TIP Before working on your project, do a test to see how the thread and needle combination works. Sew together long strips of fabric to test piecing, or appliqué a patch. Create a little quilt sandwich (top, batting, and backing) and evaluate your quilting stitches.

If you experience problems with breaking or twisting thread, the cause may be a needle mismatched to the thread type.

Troubleshooting Checklist for Needles

Your needle may be the culprit if these problems crop up while you're quilting.

● **Bearding** refers to the little white dots you see where your stitches come through the fabric. It occurs when batting comes through your fabric. Often the problem is caused by using too large a needle, a dull needle, or a needle that has a burr or nick.

● **Noisy machine stitching** (a sort of popping sound each time the needle pierces the fabric) is almost always a sign of a dull needle or damaged needle tip.

● **Skipped stitches** can be caused by a damaged or dull needle. If the needle is new, check to be sure it was inserted properly in the machine. Another problem may be a needle that is too small for the thread type. If the needle is too small, its front groove may be too shallow to protect the thread, causing stitches to be skipped.

● **Thread shredding** occurs for several reasons. The needle eye may be too small for the thread weight. If you have difficulty pulling the thread through the needle with ease, choose a needle with a larger eye. If you're working with a metallic thread, be sure to use a metallic needle specifically designed to diminish thread shredding. Metallic needles have a larger eye to reduce the friction and heat caused by the speed of the machine needle piercing the fabric.

General Tools & Supplies

It's a good idea to keep these handy items among your machine-quilting supplies.

ADHESIVES

Do you want to create a permanent bond with your fabric or one that's only temporary? Check out these adhesives to determine the best type for your quilting needs.

Basting Spray

Many brands of basting spray are available. The main point of difference is the ability to reposition the fabric. The sprays are often a good option for temporarily holding appliqués in place or for basting a small quilt or wall hanging. Follow label directions and work in a ventilated area.

Fabric Glue

Fabric glue comes in several different forms. Whether you choose a type that comes in a bottle with a needle-tip applicator or a glue-stick version, make certain the product is designed for use with fabric and is water-soluble and acid-free. When dry, fabric glue is more pliable than standard glue, and often its temporary bond allows you to reposition pieces without leaving permanent residue on your quilt.

Fusible Web

Available in prepackaged sheets or rolls, by the yard off the bolt, and as a narrow-width tape, fusible web is an iron-on adhesive that in nearly every case creates a permanent bond between layers of fabric.

Fusible web has adhesive on both sides with a paper backing on one side. It is most often used for machine appliqué. The standard version for quilting is a lightweight, paper-backed fusible web specifically designed to be stitched through. When

purchasing this product, check the label to make sure you've selected a sew-through type. If you are certain that you will not be sewing through the fused fabric (e.g., unfinished appliqué edges), you may wish to use a heavyweight, no-sew fusible web.

The manufacturer's instructions for adhering fusible web vary by brand. Follow the instructions that come with your fusible web to ensure that you're using the correct iron temperature setting, and know whether to use a dry or steam iron. These factors, along with the length of time you press, are critical to attaining a secure bond between the fusible web and the fabric.

NEEDLE THREADERS

Whether handheld or a machine attachment, this device makes getting the thread through the needle eye easier. Try several models to see which works best for your vision and coordination skills. Keep one close at hand to prevent eye strain.

PINS

Experiment with different pins, shown *above, left to right,* to determine which ones work best for your needs.

Glass-head pins allow you to press fabric pieces with pins in place and not melt the pins' heads.

Appliqué pins range from ¾" to 1¼" in length. They are designed to securely hold work in place yet prevent the sewing thread from getting snagged with each stitch.

Flat flower pins have heads shaped like flowers. The long shaft makes them easy to grab and helps the pins stay put in the fabric.

Extra-fine, or silk, pins have thin shafts and sharp points. These pins make a small hole and are easy to insert.

Safety pins (not shown) are clasps with a guard covering the point when closed. Use safety pins that are at least 1" long to pin-baste a quilt. Choose stainless-steel pins that are rust-proof and will not tarnish. There are several devices, including a spoon, that can be used to help close the pins, preventing hand fatigue. In addition, there are curved basting safety pins that slide in place without moving the quilt sandwich.

SEAM RIPPERS

Although no quilter enjoys "reverse sewing," sometimes it is necessary to remove a line of stitching. A sharp, good-quality seam ripper can make the task of removing stitches easy and cause the least damage possible to your fabric.

STABILIZERS

Stabilizers are used beneath machine appliqué or machine embroidery work to add support to the foundation fabric, helping to eliminate puckers and pulling. Stabilizers may be temporary or permanent.

Temporary stabilizers are removed after stitching is complete. Permanent stabilizers remain in the quilt or are only partially cut away after stitching. Many brands are commercially available. Two of the most common types are tear-away and water-soluble. Freezer paper also may be used as a stabilizer. Check the manufacturer's instructions on the package to select a stabilizer that is appropriate for your fabric and type of project. Experiment with a variety of stabilizers to determine which works best for you.

Batting Choices

The soft layer of material that goes between the quilt top and backing—the batting—gives a quilt dimension and definition and offers warmth. Because the best batting to use can vary from quilt to quilt, it is wise to learn the characteristics and properties of batting for the ideal match.

Your beautiful quilt top deserves a batting and backing that will enhance the finished project and be suited to its use. Historically, quiltmakers used whatever natural fibers were on hand for the quilt's middle layer or batting, but today's quilters can choose from natural and synthetic products that have a variety of characteristics.

Because batting comes in various thicknesses and fibers, it can make a quilt flat or puffy, stiff or drapable. It is available by the yard or packaged to fit standard bed sizes.

The batting you use should complement the nature and use of your finished quilt. Check package labels, talk to other quilters, and test samples to find the batting with the qualities that are important for your project.

BATTING QUALITIES

Carefully read the manufacturer's label to learn the specific qualities of a particular batting.

Bearding

Some battings beard, or have fibers that migrate through the quilt top, more than others, but any bearding is a problem when light battings are used with dark fabrics, or the reverse. Test battings with your quilt's fabrics to see if bearding will be a problem. Make sure you're not using an untreated batting. Though bearding can be attributed to a problem with your batting choice, it also could be caused by a very loosely woven fabric. Knowing what qualities to watch for can make a significant difference in your satisfaction with the finished quilt.

TIP Try black batting. It is difficult to avoid bearding when quilting large areas of black fabrics. If you're working on a dark color quilt, you may wish to consider a black batting.

Drapability

The density or sparseness of the quilting and the loft of the batting will affect the drape, or relative stiffness or softness, of the finished quilt. In general, a thinner batting and more dense quilting will result in a quilt with a softer drape. A thicker batting in a quilt that has been tied, rather than heavily quilted, will have less drape.

Grain Line

Battings can have a grain line just as fabric does. The lengthwise grain is stable and doesn't have much give, while the crosswise grain will be stretchy. In order to prevent unwanted distortion, match the batting's lengthwise grain with the backing fabric's lengthwise grain. Quilt the lengthwise grain first to limit distortion.

Loft

The thickness of a batting is referred to as its loft. Differing loft levels result in differing appearances in a finished quilt. Refer to the chart *opposite* to choose a loft compatible with your finishing method. Keep in mind that the higher the loft, the less drapability in the finished quilt.

Resiliency

Resiliency refers to the batting's ability to regain its original shape. A resilient batting, such as one made from polyester, will spring back when unfolded and resist creasing. This may be a desirable feature if you want a finished quilt with a puffy appearance. Cotton battings are less resilient and more prone to

creasing, but some of their other qualities may compensate and make their use desirable. A cotton/polyester blend batting is somewhere in between in terms of resilience.

Warmth

Cotton battings have the ability to absorb moisture, thus offering cooling comfort in the summer and a natural warmth in the winter. Wool battings provide warmth with little weight. Synthetic fibers, such as polyester, lack the breathability of natural fibers.

Washability and Shrinkage

Although polyester and wool battings resist shrinkage, cotton battings can shrink from 3 to 5 percent.

Check the package label, then decide whether or not to preshrink a batting. Some quilters prefer the puckered, antique look that comes from a batting that shrinks after it's been quilted.

SELECT YOUR BATTING

Choose a batting for your project based on the finished quilt's intended use and desired appearance.

Quilting Distance

The distance between quilting stitches is largely determined by batting qualities. The manufacturer's label will specify the maximum distance between stitching rows. If you exceed the recommended maximum distance, your batting will shift and bunch up later.

GENERAL BATTING CHARACTERISTICS

Batting Type	Advantages	Disadvantages	Characteristics
100% Cotton	Natural fiber so batting breathes. Resists fiber migration. Readily available.	May have seeds and plant residue that can release oils and stain the quilt. Often cannot be prewashed. Shrinks 3 to 5 percent when washed. May be too dense for beginning hand quilters to needle.	Can give a puckered appearance if washed after quilted. Soft, drapable. Good for experienced quilter's fine hand-quilting stitches or machine quilting.
Cotton/Polyester Blends: 80/20 50/50	Some natural fibers so batting breathes. Resists fiber migration. Easy for beginning hand quilters to needle. Readily available.	Some shrinkage, which can be avoided in many cases, if desired, by prewashing.	Low to medium loft. Drapable. Good for hand quilting and machine quilting.
Wool and Wool Blends	Natural insulator. Preshrunk. Available in black.	May have inconsistent loft. May need to be encased in cheesecloth or scrim if not bonded.	Blend of fibers from different animal breeds. Resiliency enhances quilting stitches. Soft, drapable. Good for hand and machine quilting.
Silk	Good choice for quilted garments. Does not shrink. Can be washed.	Expensive. Not widely available. Damaged by exposure to direct sunlight.	Excellent body and drape. Lightweight. Good for hand quilting and machine quilting.
Flannel	Lightweight alternative to traditional batting. Readily available.	Extreme low loft limits quilting pattern development.	100% cotton. Lightweight, thin. Good for machine quilting.
Polyester	Resilient, lightweight. Cannot be harmed by moths or mildew. Readily available. Available in black.	Synthetic fibers lack breathability.	Available in many lofts. Suitable for hand quilting and machine quilting. High loft is good for tied quilts and comforters.
Fusible	No need to prewash. Eliminates need for basting. Good choice for small projects.	Limited batting options and sizes. Adds adhesive to quilt. Difficult for hand quilters to needle.	Good for machine quilting. Eliminates need for basting.

If you know that you want to tie your finished quilt project, it is essential to select a quilt batting that allows a wide distance between stitches. A heavily quilted design will require a different choice of batting. Always refer to the package label to see if the batting you're considering is compatible with the amount of quilting you plan to do on your project.

Intended Use

Consider the intended use of your quilt. Is it a baby quilt that will be washed and dried extensively? Will it be placed on a child's bed and get pulled and tugged? Are you making a wall hanging that needs to maintain sharp, crisp corners? Are you making a quilt that you want to drape loosely over a bed and tuck beneath the pillows? Is it an heirloom project that will be used sparingly and only laundered once every few years? Is it a decorative item that will never be washed? Is it a table runner that needs to lie extremely flat? Questions such as these will help you evaluate which batting is best for your project.

Desired Appearance

Consider the fabrics in the quilt top and the backing. Are they light or dark colors? If you select a dark batting, will it show through the fabric? Would a white batting beard through the top?

Did you wash and dry your fabrics before making your quilt top, or do you want the layers to shrink as one after you've finished the project to result in an antique appearance?

What loft do you want your quilt to have? Do you want it to be big and puffy or flat and drapable?

Quilting Method

Do you plan to quilt your project by hand or machine, or are you tying it? Do you want to use perle cotton and a utility stitch to create a folk art look?

The batting type dictates the spacing between rows of quilting, so determine whether you want dense or sparse stitching before selecting a batting. The manufacturer's label will specify the maximum distance. If you exceed this distance when quilting, your batting will shift and bunch up, causing your

finished project to look uneven. If you want to tie a project, select a batting that specifies a wide distance between stitches.

Fibers

Consider whether you prefer natural or synthetic fibers, or a blend. Each choice offers different qualities. (For more information, see the General Batting Characteristics chart on *page 11.*)

Size

The quilt batting needs to be larger than the quilt top to allow for take-up during quilting and for stabilization when using a quilting frame. Add 6" to both the length and width measurements to allow an extra 3" of batting around the entire quilt.

Testing

To be sure that you'll be satisfied with your choice of batting, test it with similar fabrics, the thread, quilting technique, and washing process (if desired) used in the quilt top.

Since same-type battings from different manufacturers can vary in qualities and results, keep records of the battings you use. Your personal preferences will help you make future selections.

In addition, when looking at other quilters' finished projects, ask the makers what battings they used. The answers can help you determine the finished appearance you prefer.

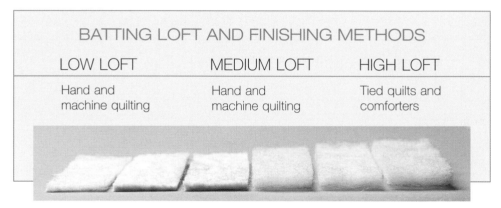

BATTING LOFT AND FINISHING METHODS

LOW LOFT	MEDIUM LOFT	HIGH LOFT
Hand and machine quilting	Hand and machine quilting	Tied quilts and comforters

TIP Is it possible to join two pieces of batting?

If your batting is too small, you can join two batting pieces to make the necessary size. Follow this process to prevent a seam-line ridge where the pieces join. Overlap the batting pieces by several inches. Rotary-cut a rolling curve through the overlapped area. Remove the excess and butt the curved edges together. Use a herringbone stitch, *right,* to join the pieces.

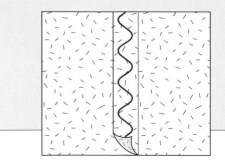

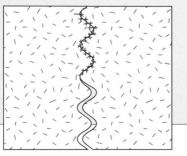

Sewing Machines

Essential to machine piecing and quilting is the sewing machine. A serviceable, basic machine in good working order is sufficient for most purposes. Newer machines offer some features and optional accessories that make piecing and quilting easier and more enjoyable. Select a brand that can have its annual maintenance and repairs handled conveniently.

Understanding your machine's features can help you avoid problems or fix them when they arise. Your machine's manual is the best resource for specific information and problem solving. Some basic information applicable to most sewing machines follows.

HOW MACHINES STITCH

Two threads coming together to hold pieces of fabric in place may appear to be magic. In reality, it takes sophisticated engineering for the two threads to create straight and decorative stitches. Understanding how thread travels through the sewing machine can be useful in preventing and solving problems.

The seams created by machine are a series of lockstitches or knots. To create lockstitches on most machines, the thread runs from the spool through tension discs and into the take-up lever. As the needle goes down into the bobbin case, the take-up lever also moves down. In the bobbin case, the bobbin hook creates a loop that interlaces with the thread coming through the needle eye. As the take-up lever and needle come back up through the fabric, the loop formed with the bobbin and needle threads is pulled up to create a stitch.

SEWING MACHINE FEATURES

Only one basic function is needed to piece and quilt by machine—sewing straight, uniform stitches to create a seam that doesn't pucker or pull the fabric. Optional features may include some or all of the following.

Adjustable Stitch Length

This feature enables you to change your stitch length from long stitches for basting to tiny stitches you might use to secure your thread at the beginning or end of a seam or quilted area. In many newer machines, this feature is expressed in millimeters (10 to 12 stitches per inch equals a 2.0- to 2.5-mm setting). If knowing the stitches per inch is important to your project, create a sample swatch and measure the number of stitches in an inch.

Adjustable Stitch Width

This feature enables you to widen zigzag and other decorative machine stitches. It can be an important feature if you enjoy crazy quilting with decorative stitches.

Zigzag and Satin Stitch

For a zigzag stitch, often used in machine appliqué, the needle swings from left to right. Adjusting the stitch length will produce stitches that are closer together. When the stitches form one against the other, filling any gaps, satin stitching is created. Often the width of the stitch also can be varied.

Needle-Down Option

Once engaged, this feature allows the needle to stop sewing in the down position every time, allowing you to pivot or adjust the fabric without losing your stitching position. If disengaged, the needle will always stop in the up position.

Adjustable Feed Dogs

The ability to drop or cover the feed dogs is important if you want to do free-motion quilting.

When the feed dogs are in the up position, *top right,* they grab onto the fabric as it moves under the presser foot.

With the feed dogs in the down position, *below,* and a darning presser foot on, you can move the fabric freely on the machine bed, controlling where and at what rate the fabric feeds beneath the presser foot.

Easily Accessible Bobbin Case

When your bobbin runs out of thread, especially if you're in the middle of a project, being able to easily change or refill it is important. Look for a machine that offers easy access to the bobbin so that you don't have to take apart the machine bed or remove the machine from the cabinet.

Extended Machine Bed Surface

An extended surface is important if you do not have your machine in a cabinet with the arm in line with the cabinet surface and you're piecing or quilting large projects. Some portable machines come with a snap-on or slide-on tray that extends the bed of the machine. You also may purchase a surround that is customized to fit around the arm of your sewing machine to extend the work area. The larger, level work surface prevents the fabric from pulling and stretching under its own weight as you work with it.

Knee-Lift Presser Foot

This feature enables you to lift and lower the presser foot by pressing your knee on a bar that extends down from the machine front. It can be especially helpful when you need both hands free to hold your fabric.

SEWING-MACHINE ACCESSORIES

Many machines come with a kit of standard accessories. Some have optional accessories you can purchase. There also are a number of generic sewing accessories designed to work with a variety of machine models. Knowing your model brand and number when purchasing generic accessories is helpful, as the packaging often states the machines and brands with which the accessories will work.

Straight-Stitch Throat Plate

A straight-stitch throat plate, *top right,* has a small, round hole for the needle to pass through, rather than the larger opening of a standard throat plate. This smaller opening allows less area for the sewing machine to take in or "swallow" the fabric as it is being stitched and results in more uniform stitches.

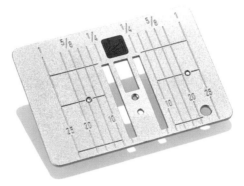

Additional Accessory Feet

Besides choosing needles and threads appropriate to your project, a couple other tools will make your machine quilting more successful. Personal preference dictates the use of many of the optional accessories.

An array of specialty feet, including open-toe appliqué and darning (used for free-motion quilting), *below,* cording, and binding feet, are available for a variety of machines. (Specific information on two types of specialty feet follows.) Check with your sewing machine's manufacturer for a complete list, or check the packaging of generic accessory feet to determine which models might be compatible with your machine.

Open-Toe Appliqué Foot

Darning Foot

¼" FOOT

Some machines allow you to reposition the needle so that it's ¼" from the edge of the standard presser foot. In addition, many machine models offer a special ¼" presser foot. With this foot and the needle in the standard position, the edge of the foot serves as the seam guide. For piecing, it is a useful accessory as you can watch only the edge of the fabric along the presser foot edge; you don't need to watch or mark a line along the throat plate or machine bed.

WALKING OR EVEN-FEED FOOT

This foot evenly feeds multiple layers of fabric and batting for machine quilting, effectively providing feed dogs for the upper fabrics to work in conjunction with the feed dogs on the machine bed. Some sewing machines come with a built-in dual-feed system, eliminating the need for a special foot. Other machines have brand-specific walking feet, while still others will accept a generic walking foot.

Use quilt clips, or bicycle clips, to secure the rolled-up edges of a large quilt you are machine-quilting. These will help you better control the bulk of the quilt as you move it around while stitching.

Adjusting Tension

When tension is balanced, stitches appear on both sides of the fabric without loops, surface knots, or broken thread.

For most piecing, your machine's tension will not need to be adjusted. Tension problems tend to be more prevalent when you're sewing with fabrics of different weights, heavy or decorative threads, or specialty needles. As with all sewing machine adjustments, check your machine's manual first when attempting to solve a tension problem.

Adjusting Upper Thread Tension

When a "bird's nest" of thread appears either on top of or underneath your fabric, the likely culprit is your upper thread tension. To determine what to correct, follow these guidelines:

If loops appear on the underside of the fabric, the upper thread tension may be too loose.

If knots appear on top of the fabric, the upper tension may be too tight.

Before adjusting the machine's tension dial, check to be sure your machine is properly threaded. If the presser foot was

lowered as you were threading your machine, it is likely the upper thread is not between the tension discs inside the machine. Or you may have missed one of the tension guides or the take-up lever. Simply raise the presser foot and rethread your machine.

If the problem still occurs, you may need to adjust the upper tension dial. If your tension is too tight, adjust the dial to a lower number. If the upper thread tension is too loose, adjust the dial to a higher number. Refer to your machine's manual for specific instructions about making tension dial adjustments.

Adjusting Bobbin Thread Tension

Although many machines allow you to adjust the upper thread tension, the bobbin thread tension is generally set by the machine's manufacturer. It doesn't usually need to be adjusted unless you're working with decorative or specialty threads (see Extra Bobbin Case on page 16).

If your bobbin thread is knotting up on the underside of your fabric, try removing the bobbin and reloading it, making sure to properly insert the thread through the bobbin tension slots as directed in your sewing machine's manual.

In some cases, you may need to try threading your bobbin thread through the hole in the bobbin case "finger" to increase the tension. Your machine manual will have instructions for this procedure if it is an option on your machine.

Knowing what affects the tension on your particular machine is critical for professional, satisfying results.

Ready-to-Sew Machine Checklist

- Machine in good working order
- Foot pedal and machine plugged in
- New needle in correct size for project
- Correct presser foot
- Bobbin wound
- Threading done properly
- Tension adjusted

Bobbins

For general piecing and quilting, use the same type of thread in the bobbin as in the top of the machine. Metallic and decorative threads are the exceptions (see pages 5 and 6). Trying to save money by using a less expensive or different type of thread in the bobbin can lead to tension difficulties.

Use bobbins that are specifically designed for your machine.

There are two basic types of bobbin mechanisms. The first is a front-loading bobbin, *below,* in which a filled bobbin fits into a bobbin case that then snaps into the opening on the front of the machine.

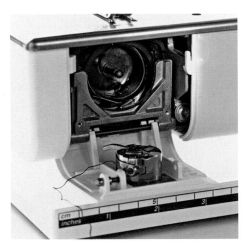

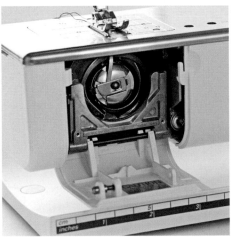

The second type of bobbin mechanism is the top-loading, or drop-in, bobbin, *below.* This type usually does not have a separate bobbin case. Instead, the filled bobbin simply drops into the bobbin casing in the bed of the

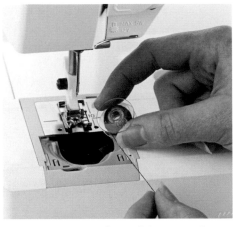

machine, usually in front of the presser foot.

Winding Bobbins

For large projects, keep multiple bobbins filled by winding several at one sitting.

Follow your machine manufacturer's directions for bobbin winding. Be sure to start the thread in the correct direction,

> Choosing a bobbin thread? For general piecing and quilting, use the same type of thread on the bobbin as is in the top of the machine (except with metallic or decorative threads). Trying to save money by using a less expensive or different type of thread on the bobbin can lead to tension difficulties.

and wind it at a speed that allows for even filling. Winding your bobbin at too fast a speed can stretch the thread, resulting in a puckered seam.

Disposable, prewound bobbins are another option, depending on what your machine will accept and what your project requires.

Extra Bobbin Case

The bobbin case that came with your machine has been factory set for sewing with basic threads. If you plan to sew with specialty threads, consider purchasing an additional bobbin case (if your machine accepts one) for use with decorative or thicker threads.

You will need to adjust the tension for these threads by turning the screw on the bobbin case's tension spring. Turn it to the left to loosen the tension and to the right to tighten the tension.

For heavy or thick threads, the tension generally needs to be loosened, and this should be accomplished in less than two complete rotations of the screw. Work over a bowl, box, or plastic bag in case the screw comes out.

Always sew a test sample after adjusting the screw.

Place a dot of nail polish or permanent marker on the second case to designate it as the case that has had its tension adjusted.

If you only have one bobbin case, make notes in your machine's manual to indicate changes in screw or tension settings when using different threads. For example, you might write "left 1½ turns for No. 5 perle cotton."

Your Work Space

Although quilting may seem like a sedentary activity, it takes energy, and the repetitive actions can stress joints and muscles. To keep sewing comfortably, follow a few simple tips for posture and position.

POSTURE

Be aware of your body posture. A straight back with your head and neck aligned and feet flat on the floor gives you the most support. Sitting or working at awkward angles and performing repetitive motions create situations that can cause injuries.

90 DEGREES

Keep this angle in mind whenever you sit down to perform a task.

Your back and legs should be at a 90° angle. Your upper and lower legs should form a 90° angle at your knees. When your feet are flat on the floor, your ankles will also be at a 90° angle.

Next, look at your arms. Your elbows should be at a 90° angle with your forearms parallel to the work surface. Keep your elbows close to your sides and your shoulders straight.

TABLE OR LARGE WORK SURFACE

A large work surface allows you to lay out long yardages of fabric when cutting or to handle a medium- to large-size quilt for basting. In addition, a large surface can give you room to spread out a project for machine quilting, preventing the project from dragging or pulling, which can result in uneven stitches.

ADJUST THE WORK SURFACE

Once you have determined your 90° positions, raise or lower your work surface and/or chair in order to hold these positions and work comfortably. If you raise your chair so your arms are at the work surface, you may not be able to keep your feet flat on the floor. Put a sturdy box or platform step under your feet so your knees and ankles stay at their 90° angles.

There are several products available at quilt shops and fabric stores that can adjust the tilt of your sewing machine or foot pedal to make it more comfortable to use and easier for you to see the machine bed. Many quilters find these products ease the stress and strain on their bodies when they sew for extended periods. If possible, sit down and try the products at the shop to see if they would aid in making your work space more comfortable.

Give yourself time. If you have been working at awkward angles, your body may have adapted and it may feel strange when you adjust your posture. Stay with the correct posture and you will benefit in the long run.

Align your cutting surface to hip height to eliminate the need to bend over and unnecessarily put strain on your back and shoulder muscles.

If you're rotary cutting, use sharp rotary blades and rulers with nonskid material to decrease the amount of pressure needed to cut fabric, thus reducing the strain on your body.

DESIGN WALL

Having a vertical surface on which to lay out fabric choices can help you visualize how they might look in a quilt. For a permanent or portable design wall, cover foam core or board insulation with a napped material, such as felt or flannel, that will hold small fabric pieces in place. Some designers use the flannel backing of a vinyl tablecloth which can be rolled up between projects or hung on a hanger.

LIGHTING

Quilting requires overall lighting and nonglare directional lighting to avoid eyestrain and produce high-quality results. Review your quilting areas for lighting, and invest in the appropriate fixtures to eliminate the headaches and vision problems that can result from eyestrain.

Specialty lamps and bulbs designed specifically for quilters are available at quilt shops. Some are designed to more accurately reflect fabric colors, filtering out excess yellow and blue tones that household bulbs can cast. These can be helpful when you are selecting fabric combinations for your quilts, especially if your quilting area does not have abundant natural daylight.

KEEP MOVING FOR PERSONAL COMFORT

Though it's easy to get lost in your quilting, it is important to your overall health to pause for a few minutes every hour to step away from your sewing machine or quilting frame and stretch. If you take time to reposition yourself periodically, you can reduce muscle fatigue and eyestrain, and enjoy several hours of quilting at a time. Speak with your health care provider about specific exercises that can help strengthen your neck, back, shoulders, arms, wrists, and hands.

Checklist for Healthy Quilting

- Avoid reaching up to the work surface.
- Sit up straight.
- Avoid reaching over or out to the work surface (keep elbows at your side).
- Take 10-minute breaks every hour.
- Drink extra water.

Learning the Technique

ONCE YOU'VE FINISHED YOUR QUILT TOP, it's time to layer it with the batting and backing so the process of quilting can begin. The quilting designs you choose can enhance the beauty, intricacy, or simplicity of your quilt. Knowing the hows and whys of this part of quiltmaking will assist you in making the right choices.

Marking the Quilt Top

Quilting designs generally are marked on a quilt top before it's layered with batting and a backing. First select a marking method according to your project; several options follow. Then select the appropriate marking tool, keeping in mind that some marking tools are more permanent than others (see pages 3–4 for more information).

Secure your quilt top to a large, flat work surface with tape or clips to prevent shifting. To begin, position your quilting design in the center of your quilt top. Reposition your design and quilt top as needed to mark the entire quilt center or quilt top. Before marking your borders, see Adjusting Border Designs to Fit on page 27 for more information.

USING A TRACING METHOD

There are several tracing methods to choose from when you wish to transfer a quilting design to a quilt top. Because these methods involve placing a light source behind the layered quilting design and quilt top, tracing works best on small- to medium-size projects.

To better see how a precut stencil's design will look when it's stitched, use a pencil to lightly trace through the stencil's cutout design onto tracing paper.

Light Bulb and Glass-Top Table

1. Place a bright light beneath a glass-top table. Or pull apart a table that accommodates leaves and place a piece of glass or clear acrylic over the opening.

2. Tape the quilting design to the top of the glass. Secure the quilt top over the design, and trace the design onto the fabric.

Light Box

1. Tape the quilting design to a light box. Turn on the light source.

2. Secure the quilt top over the design, and trace the design onto the fabric.

What's a quilt sandwich? Quilters use this term to describe the quilt top, batting, and backing once they've been layered together.

Sunny Window

1. Tape the quilting design to a clean, dry window on a sunny day.

2. Tape the quilt top over the design, and trace the design onto the fabric.

USING STENCILS AND TEMPLATES

1. To transfer a quilting design using a stencil or template, place the pattern on the quilt top and secure it in place with tape or weights.

2. Mark the pattern on the fabric.

USING TEAR-AWAY PATTERNS

1. Mark the quilting design on tracing paper, tissue paper, or tear-away stabilizer. You will need to make one pattern for each time the design will be used on the quilt top.

2. Baste or pin the pattern to the quilt top. Quilt along the design lines through both the paper and the quilt.

3. Gently tear the paper patterns away from the quilt top.

USING PERFORATED PATTERNS

1. Mark the quilting design on sturdy paper. Sew over the paper's design lines with a sewing machine and an unthreaded needle (or trace the lines with a needle-pointed tracing wheel).

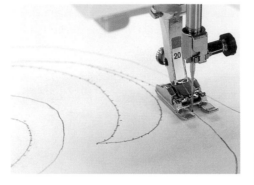

2. Secure the quilt top to a firm surface, then secure the perforated pattern to the quilt top. Go over the perforations with chalk, pounce, or stamping powder.

USING TAPE

Use quilter's tape, painter's tape, or masking tape to mark straight-line quilting designs. (See page 4 for more information on tapes.) The tape can be put in place before or after the quilt layers are sandwiched together. Reposition the tape as needed until the quilting is complete; then remove it.

To avoid a sticky residue on your fabric, do not leave tape in place for an extended period of time.

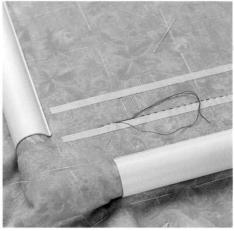

What's the difference between a stencil and a template? Both are patterns. A template is a pattern created by marking around a shape. A stencil is a pattern through which a design is transferred. Stencils have slits in the surface for you to mark through, while a template's outer edge is in the shape of its design. You can make your own stencils and templates or purchase them ready-made at a quilt shop.

Creating the "Sandwich"

THE BATTING

Once the quilt top is marked, it's time to prepare the batting.

1. Remove the batting from its packaging and spread it out on a large, flat surface to allow the folds to relax overnight. Or fluff the batting in a clothes dryer for a few minutes on an air-dry setting to remove wrinkles.

2. Trim the batting so that it's at least 3" larger on all sides than the quilt top.

THE LAYERS

Take your time layering the quilt top, batting, and backing. Being careful at this point will save frustration when quilting. It is best to assemble the layers on a large, flat surface where the entire quilt top can be spread out.

1. If the quilt backing is pieced, press all the seam allowances open. This will prevent added bulk when you are quilting.

2. Place the quilt backing wrong side up on a large, flat surface. Tape, clip, or otherwise secure the quilt backing to the work surface.

3. Center and smooth the batting atop the quilt backing. If desired, baste the batting and backing together with a single large cross-stitch in the center to prevent the layers from shifting. (This is especially important when working on a surface that's smaller than your quilt top.)

4. Center the quilt top right side up on top of the batting. To be sure that it is centered, fold it in half with the right side inside. Align the center fold of the quilt with the center of the batting, then unfold the quilt top and smooth out any wrinkles.

5. To check that you have not stretched the quilt top out of alignment during the layering process, place a square ruler in one corner, *top right*. The edges of the ruler should be flush with the quilt top's edges. If the quilt is squared up, pin the border in that corner to hold it in place. Repeat in the remaining three corners. If the quilt top is not square, repeat step 4, taking care not to stretch it.

6. Pin or baste all the layers together, beginning at the center. Be careful not to shift the layers, and work toward the edges, smoothing the fabrics as you go. (Refer to the basting instructions that follow for additional information.)

PIN BASTING

Machine quilters generally pin-baste because it is easier to remove pins rather than basting threads from underneath stitching.

1. Pin the three layers together with rust-proof safety pins, making a horizontal line and a vertical line through the center of the quilt sandwich to form quadrants on the quilt top.

2. Add pins over the surface of the quilt top at 3" to 4" intervals.

SPRAY BASTING

Basting sprays are best for small projects, such as wall hangings. Follow the manufacturer's directions to adhere the layers to one another. Take care not to overspray, which can lead to a gummy buildup on your needle. (See page 9 for more information on basting sprays.)

Machine Quilting

Though some believe machine quilting to be a modern method, there are examples that date back to the early days of sewing machines. With the versatility of today's sewing machines, as well as the expanded availability of long-arm quilting machines outside the commercial market, machine quilting continues to grow in popularity. With practice and perseverance, you can create keepsake-quality quilts with your sewing machine.

Machine-quilting stitches are continuous and even, giving a quilt a precise look. Just as in hand quilting, practice pays when it comes to machine quilting. If you're new to the process, start with straight lines that are stitched from edge to edge to avoid lots of stopping and starting. Then try grid patterns and more intricate designs. As you gain proficiency and become more comfortable working with your sewing machine in this way, you'll be motivated to do more, which will lead to even better results.

> To avoid having the entire quilt beneath the sewing-machine arm at one time, begin working at the center of a quilt and work toward one edge. Complete half of the quilt top, then turn it around and quilt the other half, keeping in mind any directional motifs you may be stitching.

MACHINE-QUILTING SETUP

Make sure your machine is clean and in good working order. Arrange a large, flat working surface that's even with the bed (throat plate) of the machine. It is important that the work surface support the weight of the quilt to prevent pulling and shifting of layers. Make certain the quilt layers are securely basted.

Be sure that you're comfortably seated, with the machine in a position that allows you to see and reach without straining your shoulders, arms, and hands.

For straight-line machine quilting, set up your machine with a walking (even-feed) foot and a straight-stitch throat plate. (Free-motion machine quilting requires a different presser foot. See Free-Motion Quilting on page 24 for information.) Set the stitch length for 8 to 12 stitches per inch.

The style of needle most often used is a sharp 80/12. You can experiment with smaller needles (75/11 or 70/10) if you feel the holes left in the fabric by the needle are too large.

The most common thread choice is 50-weight, three-ply, 100% cotton machine-quilting thread. If you want the finished stitches to be invisible, use very fine, transparent, nylon, monofilament thread (.004 mm) in the needle and lightweight cotton or bobbin-fill thread in the bobbin.

STARTING AND STOPPING MACHINE-QUILTING STITCHES

1. At the beginning of a line of stitching, pull the bobbin thread to the quilt top. Lock the stitches by setting the machine's stitch length to the shortest setting and sewing forward about ¼".

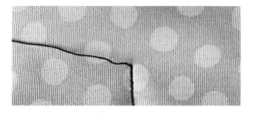

2. Stop sewing, reset the stitch length to the preferred setting, and continue sewing.

3. To finish a line of stitching, return the machine's stitch length to the shortest setting, and sew forward about ¼".

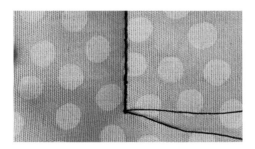

4. Raise the presser foot, remove the quilt, and clip the threads.

What is a long-arm quilting machine?
A long-arm quilting machine holds a quilt taut on a frame, which allows the quilter to see and work on a larger portion of the quilt at one time than would be possible with a standard sewing machine. The machine head moves freely, allowing the operator to quilt in all directions. These machines are most often used by professional machine quilters.

IN-THE-DITCH MACHINE QUILTING

Quilting "in the ditch" means stitching just inside a seam line, *below, top.*

The stitches disappear into the seam, which makes a patch, block, or motif stand out from its background, *below, bottom.* It is one of the easiest methods to do by machine.

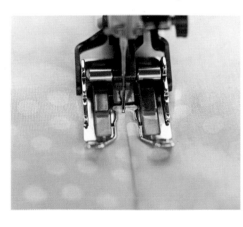

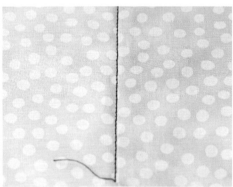

1. Attach a walking (even-feed) foot. Find the lengthwise center seam line of the basted quilt sandwich. With the needle just to one side of that seam line, sew along it from border to border.

2. Turn the quilt crosswise; adjust all the layers so they are smooth. Stitch the crosswise center seam in the same manner.

3. Return the quilt sandwich to the lengthwise direction and stitch in the ditch along the seam lines in a quadrant to the right of the center seam, working from the center outward toward the border.

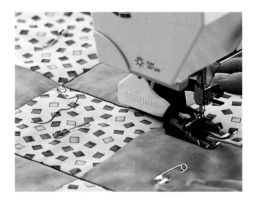

4. Turn the quilt and stitch in the ditch on the seam lines in a quadrant on the opposite side of the center line, again working from the center outward toward the border.

5. Repeat in the remaining two quadrants of the quilt.

CHANNEL OR GRID MACHINE QUILTING

When you want straight lines that do not necessarily follow the seam lines, you can do channel or grid quilting.

Channel Quilting

Channel quilting consists of parallel rows of straight lines going in one direction across a quilt top. Some sewing machines come with a quilting bar that attaches to the machine to serve as a guide for evenly spaced rows. Use the bar when your quilting rows are farther apart than a presser-foot width or when the guides on your machine bed are covered. The bar is particularly useful when you're quilting straight rows across a large project.

> **Avoid force-feeding the quilt into the machine.** Feed the fabric up to the walking foot gently, but don't push the fabric ahead. Pushing it causes tucks at the crossing of each seam. Try not to stretch the quilt top or force it under the needle as that will cause the batting to pull, distorting the finished quilt.

When channel quilting, you need to mark at least the center line on your quilt top before you begin stitching. Follow the steps described in In-the-Ditch Machine Quilting on page 23, anchoring the center line first, then stitching each half of the quilt. Work from the center outward toward the border until an area is completely quilted.

Grid Quilting

Grid quilting involves stitching parallel rows of straight lines in two directions across a quilt top. When quilting in a grid, you need to mark at least the horizontal and vertical center lines on your quilt top before you begin stitching. The same quilting bar used for channel quilting can help keep rows straight for grid quilting. Follow the steps described in In-the-Ditch Machine Quilting on page 23, anchoring the center lines first, then stitching quadrant by quadrant until finished.

FREE-MOTION QUILTING

Free-motion machine quilting is used to stitch curved lines and designs. In free-motion machine quilting, you sew with the machine's feed dogs in the down position in order to control the stitch length and direction.

It takes practice to achieve the steadiness and speed control necessary for creating small, uniform-size stitches. Start with a small project and simple quilting designs, and work up to a larger quilt with more complicated designs.

1. Attach a darning foot to your sewing machine, and drop or cover the feed dogs.

2. Position the basted quilt sandwich beneath the darning foot. Bring the bobbin thread to the surface of the quilt top.

3. Lower the presser foot. *Note: Even though the darning foot does not touch the quilt top when the presser foot is lowered, lowering it before stitching will help prevent the quilt from "jumping" up and down as the needle goes in and out; doing so also engages the tension discs, which will make your stitches more even and taut.*

Hold both the needle and the bobbin threads in one hand. Take three to six stitches in the same area to lock the stitches.

Move the quilt sandwich in the direction you wish to go. (With the feed dogs down, the fabric layers will not move unless you move them.)

4. Clip the thread ends.

5. Begin stitching, moving the quilt sandwich slowly with the machine stitching at a medium-fast, constant speed. Glide the fabric layers in the direction they need to go. Do not turn the quilt. Because the feed dogs are lowered, you will be able to move the quilt sandwich freely from side to side and front to back. Use as little hand pressure as possible to move and control the quilt.

6. End your stitching by taking three to six stitches in the same area to lock the stitches. Remove the quilt top from the machine and clip the thread ends.

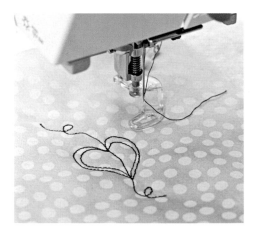

Some machine quilters wear special gloves with grippers on the palms for better control as they shift the quilt on the machine bed when quilting.

FOLDING A LARGE PROJECT FOR MACHINE QUILTING

When you're working on a large quilt, it can be difficult to control the bulk of many fabric layers, especially between the needle and the inside of the machine arm. Many machine quilters find it is easier to roll the project and work on small areas at a time.

1. Evenly roll or fold up opposite sides of the quilt sandwich. Secure the sides as desired. *Note: Quilt shops often carry clips specially designed for this purpose.*

2. Evenly roll or fold up a remaining quilt side, again securing as desired.

3. Place the project beneath the needle and presser foot, and begin quilting.

4. Reroll or refold the layered quilt sandwich to stitch new areas.

MACHINE-QUILTING DESIGNS

Machine quilting can produce almost a limitless number of designs. Besides the straight lines and intricate curves described on previous pages, there are quilting designs created specifically for sewing machines. The advantage of these designs is that they involve minimal starting and stopping. Arrows on the stitching patterns indicate the direction you should sew. For inspiration, see Quilt as Desired beginning on page 26.

To decide if your quilting thread contrasts or blends the way you wish, practice your quilting designs on quilt sandwiches made from the same fabrics used in your quilt. If the color is not right, experiment with thread a shade lighter or darker.

If you're assembling a quilt on a table that is smaller than the quilt backing, center the fabric on the table top so equal lengths hang down on each side like a tablecloth.

Let the large work surface around your sewing machine support the weight of the quilt as you machine-quilt. Avoid letting the quilt drop to the floor and create drag. If you have limited work surface, adjust an ironing board to the height of your sewing machine bed to help support the quilt's weight.

Quilt as Desired

Instructions for making a quilt generally come with detailed steps, numerous patterns, and helpful diagrams. How you should quilt the project often goes unsaid. Many quiltmakers simply quilt in the ditch or in an allover meandering pattern because they don't know what else to do.

If "quilt as desired" is your only instruction, those three words needn't leave you wondering how to proceed. Instead, look at them as an invitation to begin the next phase of completing a fabulous quilt project.

QUESTIONS TO ASK

Take some time and ask yourself the following questions. They'll help you make decisions on how to quilt your project.

Is this a quilt I hope will remain in my family for several generations?

When creating an heirloom quilt, consider quilting the project with elaborate designs and intricate details. For other projects, simple quilting designs that are easy to complete may be more appropriate.

Is this quilt going to be laundered often?

Select machine quilting for quilts that will receive lots of use.

How much time do I have to complete this quilt?

Save hand quilting for projects where you can afford to invest the time. If time is limited but you want to hand-quilt a project, select easy-to-do designs and motifs.

What's my preferred quilting method, by hand or by machine?

Just as when selecting a project, if you're excited about the process you've chosen, you'll be more likely to finish it successfully. Whether you want to hand- or machine-quilt may also affect your choice of a quilting

design, as some lend themselves better to one technique than the other. For example, if you're going to machine-quilt, a continuous line design is often the best option since there will be less starting and stopping.

Do I want my quilting stitches to be visible in the quilt top?

Whether quilting by hand or machine, save intricate, close quilting for projects that will showcase the stitching and more basic designs for those with busier fabrics and more pieces where it's likely the quilting stitches won't show.

Does this quilt have a traditional, folk art, or contemporary mood?

Sometimes the feel of a quilt will drive the quilting design. For example, a traditional quilt may call for a feathered wreath design, but a folk art quilt may look best with big stitches quilted in perle cotton.

FINDING INSPIRATION

Ideas for quilting motifs and designs don't have to be limited to the precut stencils, templates, and books of quilting designs available at your local quilt shop. Look around you for inspiration.

One way to generate designs is to think about your project's theme. For example, if you're making a Christmas quilt, consider holiday-related items, such as ornaments, strings of lights, trees, holly, garland, mittens, snowflakes, reindeer, and stockings, as potential quilting motifs. Evaluate the possibilities based on difficulty and where they might work best on your quilt.

A round ornament could be stitched as a simple circle, for instance, while a reindeer would probably require a stencil. A wavy line with occasional loops could represent garland on a narrow inner border.

Another place to find a quilting design is within the quilt's fabrics. Are there motifs in

one of the prints, such as oak leaves or flowers, that could work as a the quilting design?

The architecture of buildings can provide numerous concepts. For instance, the exteriors of old brick buildings often show interesting grid arrangements that can be translated into quilting patterns. Wrought-iron fences and gates might suggest beautiful scrollwork, perfect for border designs. Door arches, moldings, or pressed-tin ceilings may offer ideas for your next medallion-style quilt.

Even household items, such as picture frames, jewelry, and kitchen tiles, can produce quilting design ideas. The bubbles in an aquarium, for example, may suggest the perfect pattern for a goldfish quilt.

Examine both new and old quilts that you like. Ask yourself: Why do I like this quilt? What about it appeals to me? Is it the pieced or appliquéd pattern? Is it the colors? Or is it the quilting design that brings it all together?

QUILTING TERMINOLOGY

Understanding some general quilting terms will help you select a design for your next project.

Allover designs, particularly geometrics, can be stitched over an entire quilt without regard to shapes or fabrics. Allover designs can be quilted from either the top side or the backing.

Backgrounds and fillers cover open interior spaces, such as setting squares, circles, or hearts, with stitching. You can stitch squares, diamonds, clamshells, or other small regular shapes. You also can stitch these shapes in the background outside an appliqué or quilted motif. The closely spaced lines of a filler tend to flatten the area, creating a low-relief, textured appearance.

Big, or utility, stitches require a heavier thread, such as perle cotton, and a large hand stitch. They result in a folk art appearance.

Echo quilting involves stitching multiple lines that follow the outline of an appliqué or other design element, repeating its shape. The evenly spaced quilting lines should be ¼" to ½" apart. You can use echo quilting to completely fill a background.

In the ditch means stitching just inside a seam line. The stitches disappear into the seam, which makes a patch, block, or motif stand out from its background. It's an easy method to do by machine.

Outline quilting is done ¼" from a seam line or edge of an appliqué shape, just past the extra thickness of the pressed seam allowance. If you want to quilt closer to a seam line, choose the side opposite the pressed seam allowance.

Stippling, also called allover meandering or puzzle quilting, can be stitched by hand or machine. It involves random curves, straight rows of regularly placed stitches (lined up or staggered), or random zigzags. For the best effect, stippling should be closely spaced.

BORDER DESIGNS AND BALANCE

Borders and quilt centers are usually quilted separately. Although one option is to leave the border unquilted, doing so tends to make the final project look unbalanced. That's also the result if the border quilting doesn't fit the rest of the project.

Don't skimp on quilting in the borders; try to keep the amount of quilting equal to the rest of the quilt.

To balance your quilting designs, include the borders when you begin thinking about quilting designs for your blocks. Think about what will coordinate with or complement the quilting designs you've selected for the rest of the quilt top.

If you've selected a particular motif or design for the quilt center, is there a way to continue that same motif or a variation of it in the border? For example, if the blocks are quilted with a simple flower, can it be repeated in the border, perhaps adding a connecting vine-and-leaf pattern? If you are crosshatching the blocks, can you crosshatch through the border as well?

As you select your quilting designs, evaluate the fabric used in the border. Is it a solid or a subtle print that will really show off a quilting design? Or is the fabric so busy it will hide any type of quilting?

If you have a solid inner border and a print outer border, you may want to quilt a recognizable pattern in the solid border, where it will show up better, then crosshatch or stipple the busier fabric.

AUDITIONING DESIGNS

Once you have an idea for a border quilting design, it's best to create a paper template or tracing paper overlay to see how the design will fit in the length of your borders and how it will turn the corners. Use a temporary quilting pencil or marker to draw it on your quilt top. Always test the pencil or marker on scraps of the fabrics used in the quilt top before marking on the actual top. (See Marking the Quilt Top, which begins on page 19, for more information.)

ADJUSTING BORDER DESIGNS TO FIT

There is no single formula for success in adjusting border designs to fit a quilt. Because of the variety of factors involved—border width and length, quilting design width and repeat—the ways to adjust a border design are numerous. An important consideration as you adjust the design is the goal to have all sides and corners match. The most challenging method is to adjust the length of a continuous design. However, there are options other than adjusting a border design's width and length.

Extending the Center Design

If an overall design, such as crosshatching or stippling, is used on the quilt center, consider extending it onto the borders as shown *below*.

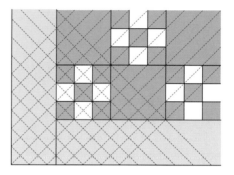

Meandering Vine Design

Try meandering a vine design along each border. When you reach the corners, be sure to turn the design in an identical manner, creating mirror images in opposite corners as shown *below*.

Repeated Block Design

Repeat a block design used in the quilt center in the border (or choose a different design), evenly spacing the design along the length as shown *below.* Pay particular attention to the direction of the motifs. You may wish to point them all in one direction if the motif has a definite top and bottom. Or point all the designs toward or away from the quilt center.

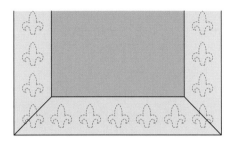

Combining Elements

If you choose a rhythmic or wavy design, such as swags or feathers, but the motifs don't fit, consider combining them with a block design at the midpoint of each border as shown by the bow motif *below.*

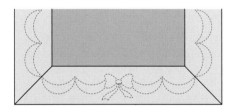

Adjusting the Length of the Design

Adjusting a continuous line design takes the most time and effort of any adjustment, but when completed, it results in a design that appears to seamlessly circle the entire quilt. The instructions that follow are for modifying a stencil design. Drawing the design first on paper (shelf liner or freezer paper) will prevent you from incorrectly marking your quilt top.

Though the steps for adjusting border designs are generally the same, how you choose to add or take out extra length so that the design fits is unique to each project.

As a rule, it's best not to modify a design at the corners. Instead, adjust the design somewhere near, but not at, the midpoint.

1. Cut two lengths of paper, one equal in width and length to the quilt's finished side borders and one equal in width and length to the top/bottom borders. Do not include the seam allowances. (If your quilt is square, one strip will do.) Label the strips and mark the center of each.

2. Trace the stencil's corner design on the ends of each strip. Use the registration marks on the stencil to make sure your design is properly aligned on the paper border.

3. Align the center registration mark on the stencil with the midpoint marked on the border. Beginning from this point, slide the stencil between the midpoint and corner to figure how many repetitions of the design will fit. The alterations will likely be different for the side and top/bottom borders.

If the amount of design adjustment is small, you may be able to adjust a bit of length in one motif without noticeably altering the design. If the amount to be added or reduced is too great, the design will be distorted, calling attention to the motif that was squeezed or stretched to fit.

If the amount is significant, you will need to add or delete a part of several motifs to make the adjustment. When doing so, keep in mind the overall shape of the design and use the stencil as much as possible to trace the design on the paper.

4. Once you're pleased with the paper patterns, transfer the modified design to the quilt top. (See Marking the Quilt Top on page 19.)

Choose a border design that fills the border's width well, keeping in mind you don't want the quilting to go too near the seam allowance or you'll risk covering it with the binding.

Having trouble basting a large quilt without the layers shifting? Often the problem is not having a large enough work space to lay the entire quilt flat. Working on the floor is less than desirable and hard on your back. If work space is at a premium in your home, see if there's basting space at your local quilt shop, community center, or church. The large tables often found in these places can be pushed together to make a surface that's easy to work around without having to adjust the quilt.

USE THOSE "LEFTOVERS" Want to work on improving your machine quilting without practicing on an actual project? Make sandwiches from scraps of fabric and batting and practice your stitching techniques on them. This is an excellent way to use your scraps and experiment with different quilting designs and stitches before trying them on a project.

Gallery of Quilting Designs

STYMIED AT THE THOUGHT OF PLANNING A QUILTING DESIGN for your pieced quilt top? Don't be! The ideas and examples that follow are loaded with creative solutions to delight and inspire you. Some of the samples featured are quilted by machine, others by hand. Simply choose and adapt your favorites to make your finished piece an exciting, personal expression of your needlework skills.

1a

2

1b

1 The floral print backing (1a) offered the quilter a chance to outline-quilt the flower and leaf motifs by machine, which resulted in an easy overall design on the quilt top (1b).

2 Bright, playful colors called for a fun, free-motion design of loops and scallops done by machine.

A Trio of Patchwork Projects

YOU MAY HAVE A PIECED TOP THAT'S READY FOR QUILTING and have already decided to make it your first machine-quilting project. If so, consider these designs for their quilting pattern ideas. However, if you're starting from scratch, one of these three easy-to-piece projects might be the perfect place to begin.

SHERBET
Parfait

Diagonally set Snowball and Nine-Patch blocks combine to form sherbet-color stars on designer Tammy Kelly's simple wall hanging.

Photographs by Perry Struse

Materials

½ yard of solid dark pink for blocks
1 yard of pink stripe for blocks
3—¼-yard pieces of assorted purple prints for blocks and border
3—¼-yard pieces of assorted pink prints for blocks and border
⅛ yard of lime green print for blocks
⅛ yard of orange print for blocks
⅝ yard of yellow batik for blocks and setting triangles
½ yard of solid purple for binding
2½ yards of backing fabric
45×54" of quilt batting

Finished quilt top: 39×47½"
Finished block: 6" square

Quantities specified for 44/45"-wide, 100% cotton fabrics. All measurements include a ¼" seam allowance.
Sew with right sides together unless otherwise stated.

Cut the Fabrics

To make the best use of your fabrics, cut the pieces in the order that follows.

From solid dark pink, cut:
- 80—2½" squares
- 8—2⅛" squares

From pink stripe, cut:
- 20—6½" squares
- 8—2⅛" squares

From *each* assorted purple print, cut:
- 1—2½×42" strip

From *two* assorted purple prints, cut:
- 2—3×11⅛" strips for border
- 2—3×9" strips for border

From *each* assorted pink print, cut:
- 1—2½×42" strip

From *two* assorted pink prints, cut:
- 2—3×11⅛" strips for border
- 2—3×9" strips for border

From lime green print, cut:
- 1—2½×42" strip

From orange print, cut:
- 1—2½×42" strip

From yellow batik, cut:
- 4—9¾" squares, cutting each diagonally twice in an X for a total of 16 setting triangles (you'll have 2 leftover triangles)
- 2—5⅛" squares, cutting each in half diagonally for a total of 4 corner triangles
- 1—2½×42" strip

From solid purple, cut:
- 5—2½×42" binding strips

Assemble the Snowball Blocks

1. For accurate sewing lines, use a quilter's pencil to mark a diagonal line on the wrong side of the 80 solid dark pink 2½" squares. (To prevent the fabric from stretching as you draw the lines, place 220-grit sandpaper under the squares.)

2. Align a marked solid dark pink square with each corner of a pink stripe 6½" square (see Diagram 1; note the placement of the marked diagonal lines). Stitch on the marked lines; trim away the excess fabric, leaving ¼" seam allowances. Press the attached triangles open to make a Snowball block. The pieced Snowball block should still measure 6½" square, including the seam allowances. Repeat to make a total of 20 Snowball blocks.

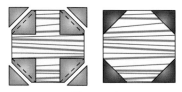

Diagram 1

Assemble the Nine-Patch Blocks

1. Aligning long edges, sew together an orange print 2½×42" strip, a purple print 2½×42" strip, and a yellow batik 2½×42" strip to make a strip set A (see Diagram 2). Press the seam allowances toward the purple print strip. Pieced strip set A should measure 6½×42", including the seam allowances. Cut the strip set into twelve 2½"-wide segments.

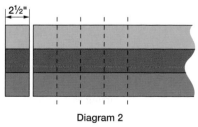

Diagram 2

2. Sew together a pink print 2½×42" strip, a lime green print 2½×42" strip, and a purple print 2½×42" strip to make a strip set B (see Diagram 3). Press the seam allowances away from the center strip. Cut the strip set into twelve 2½"-wide segments.

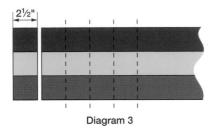

Diagram 3

3. Sew together the remaining two pink print 2½×42" strips and the remaining purple print 2½×42" strip to make a strip set C (see Diagram 4). Press the seam allowances toward the purple print strip. Cut the strip set into twelve 2½"-wide segments.

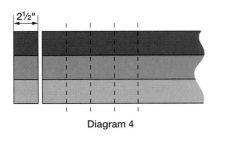

Diagram 4

4. Lay out a strip set A segment, a strip set B segment, and a strip set C segment as shown in Diagram 5. Sew together the segments to make a Nine-Patch block. Press the seam allowances toward the center segment. The Nine-Patch block should measure 6½" square, including the seam allowances. Repeat to make a total of 12 Nine-Patch blocks.

Diagram 5

Assemble the Quilt Center

1. Referring to the Quilt Assembly Diagram, *opposite,* for placement, lay out the 20 Snowball blocks, the 12 Nine-Patch blocks, and 14 yellow batik setting triangles in diagonal rows.

2. Sew together the pieces in each diagonal row. Press the seam allowances toward the Nine-Patch blocks and setting triangles. Then join the rows. Press the seam allowances in one direction.

3. Add the four yellow batik corner triangles to complete the quilt center. Press the seam allowances toward the corner triangles. The pieced quilt center should measure 34½×43", including the seam allowances.

Assemble and Add the Border

1. Repeat step 1 under Assemble the Snowball Blocks to mark the solid dark pink 2⅛" squares.

2. Align a marked solid dark pink 2⅛" square with a pink stripe 2⅛" square (see Diagram 6, *opposite*). Stitch ¼" on each side of the drawn line; cut apart on the drawn line to make two triangle units. Press the triangle units open to make two triangle-squares.

Each triangle-square should measure 1¾" square, including the seam allowances. Repeat to make a total of 16 triangle-squares.

Diagram 6

3. Referring to Diagram 7 for placement, sew together four triangle-squares in pairs. Press the seam allowances in opposite directions. Then join the pairs to make a Pinwheel block. The pieced Pinwheel block should measure 3" square, including the seam allowances. Repeat to make a total of four Pinwheel blocks.

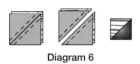

Diagram 7

4. Aligning the short edges, sew together two purple print and two pink print 3×11⅛" strips, alternating colors, to make a side border strip. Repeat to make a second side border strip.

5. Sew the side border strips to the side edges of the pieced quilt center. Press the seam allowances toward the border.

6. Again aligning the short edges, sew together two purple print and two pink print 3×9" strips, alternating colors, to make a top border strip. Repeat to make a bottom border strip.

7. Sew a Pinwheel block to each end of the strips. Sew the pieced top and bottom border strips to the top and bottom edges of the pieced quilt center to complete the quilt top. Press the seam allowances toward the border.

Complete the Quilt

1. Cut and piece the backing fabric to measure at least 3" bigger than the quilt top on all sides. Press all seam allowances open. With wrong sides together, layer the quilt top and backing fabric with the batting in between. Baste the layers.

2. Quilt as desired. An overall floral and loopy design was machine-quilted in the featured project.

3. Use the solid purple 2½×42" strips to bind the quilt according to the instructions on page 47. Follow steps 4–9.

Quilt Assembly Diagram

BONNY
Blue & White

Designer Joy Hoffman created this lively design in shades of blue and crisp white. Join the blocks in checkerboard fashion, and the piece visually spins!

Photograph by Perry Struse

Materials

1½ yards of solid white for blocks
7—½-yard pieces of solid blue in shades ranging from light to dark for blocks, borders, and binding
3 yards of backing fabric
54×66" of quilt batting

Finished quilt top: 48×60"
Finished block: 6" square

Quantities specified for 44/45"-wide, 100% cotton fabrics. All measurements include a ¼" seam allowance unless otherwise stated.

Cut the Fabrics

To make the best use of your fabrics, cut the pieces in the order that follows. The Triangle Pattern is on *page 42*. Make a template of the pattern from template plastic (see page 3 for more information).

Before cutting any fabrics, set aside the lightest blue fabric to use for the binding. From the six remaining blue fabrics, separate out the darkest blue and cut enough pieces to make 13 blocks (seven with blue stars and six with white stars). Finally, cut enough pieces from the remaining five blue fabrics to make 10 blocks each (five with blue stars and five with white stars from each blue fabric).

From solid white, cut:
- 124—2×3½" rectangles
- 252 of Triangle Pattern

From *each* of five solid blues, cut:
- 20—2×3½" rectangles
- 40 of Triangle Pattern

From darkest solid blue, cut:
- 28—2×3½" rectangles
- 52 of Triangle Pattern

Assemble the Star Blocks

1. For one blue star block you'll need four blue triangles of the same fabric, four white triangles, and four white 2×3½" rectangles.

2. Sew together a blue triangle and a white triangle to make a blue star point (see Diagram 1). Press the seam allowance toward the blue triangle. The pieced star point should measure 2×3½", including the seam allowances. Repeat to make a total of four blue star points.

Diagram 1

3. Sew a white 2×3½" rectangle to the white long edge of each blue star point to make four blue star point units (see Diagram 2).

Diagram 2

4. Referring to Diagram 3 for placement, lay out the four blue star point units in two horizontal rows. Sew together the units in each row. Press the seam allowances in opposite directions. Then join the rows to make a star block. Press the seam allowance open. The pieced blue star block should measure 6½" square, including seam allowances.

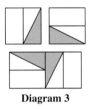

Diagram 3

5. Repeat steps 1–4 to make a total of 31 blue star blocks.

6. For one white star block you'll need four blue triangles and four blue 2×3½" rectangles of the same fabric and four white triangles.

7. Repeat Step 2 to make a total of four white star points. Sew a blue 2×3½" rectangle to the blue long edge of each white star point to make four white star point units (see Diagram 4).

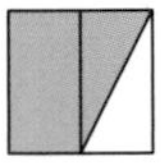

Diagram 4

8. Repeat Step 4 using four white star point units to piece a white star block (see Diagram 5).

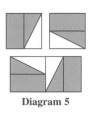

Diagram 5

9. Repeat steps 6–8 to make a total of 32 white star blocks.

Assemble the Center

Referring to the Quilt Assembly Diagram, *right*, lay out the star blocks in nine horizontal rows. Sew together the blocks in each row. Press the seam allowances in one direction, alternating the direction in each row. Join the rows to complete the quilt center. The pieced quilt center should measure 42½×54½", including seam allowances.

Cut and Add Borders

From solid medium-light blue, cut:
● 1—3½×42½" border strip
From solid blue, cut:
● 1—3½×42½" border strip
From solid medium-dark blue, cut:
● 2—3½×42" border strips
From solid dark blue, cut:
● 2—3½×42" border strips
From solid darkest blue, cut:
● 4—3½" squares

1. Sew a solid medium-light blue 3½×42½" border strip to the top edge and a solid blue 3½×42½" border strip to the bottom edge of the pieced quilt center. Press the seam allowances toward the blue border.

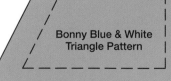

Bonny Blue & White
Triangle Pattern

2. Piece the solid medium-dark blue 3½×42" border strips to make the following:
● 1—3½×54½" border strip

3. Piece the solid dark blue 3½×42" border strips to make the following:
● 1—3½×54½" border strip

4. Sew a solid darkest blue 3½" square to each end of the solid medium-dark blue 3½×54½" border strip and the solid dark blue 3½×54½" border strip to make two pieced border units. Sew a pieced border unit to each side edge of the pieced quilt center to complete the top of the quilt. Press the seam allowances toward the blue border.

Complete the Quilt
From lightest solid blue, cut:
● 6—2½×42" binding strips

Layer the quilt top, batting, and backing, according to the instructions under Complete the Quilt on *page 47*. Referring to the photo on *page 41*, quilt as desired. Use the lightest solid blue 2½×42" strips to bind the quilt, following steps 4–9 on *page 47*.

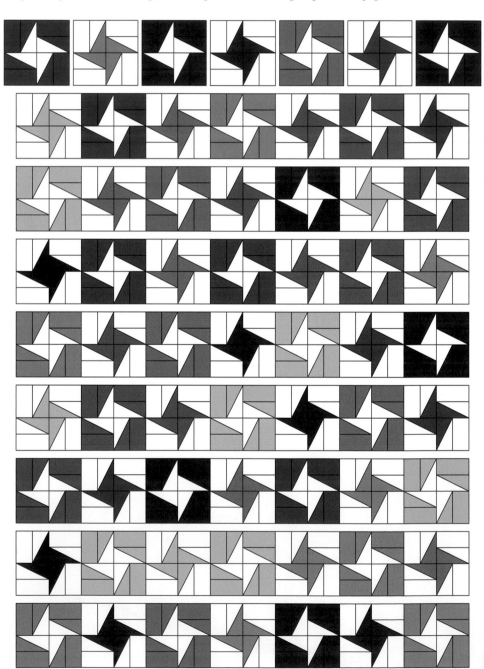

Quilt Assembly Diagram

FLY AWAY
Home

Contrasting colors imply movement in this easy-to-piece quilt of Rail Fence and Wild Goose Chase blocks from designers Anne Moscicki and Linda Wyckoff-Hickey.

Photographs by Perry Struse

Materials

2⅛ yards total of assorted navy blue
  prints for Wild Goose Chase blocks
1⅛ yards total of assorted tan prints for
  Wild Goose Chase blocks
1⅛ yards total of assorted light blue
  prints for Wild Goose Chase blocks
3½ yards total of assorted dark red,
  green, rust, and purple prints for
  Rail Fence blocks
1¼ yards of dark blue print for inner
  border and binding
1¾ yards of blue print for outer border
7¼ yards of backing fabric
92" square of quilt batting

Finished quilt top: 86" square
Finished block: 12" square

Quantities specified for 44/45"-wide, 100%
cotton fabrics. All measurements include a
¼" seam allowance. Sew with right sides
together unless otherwise stated.

Cut the Fabrics

To make the best use of your fabrics, cut the
pieces in the order that follows.

From assorted navy blue prints, cut:
● 224—3½" squares
From assorted tan prints, cut:
● 56—3½×6½" rectangles
From assorted light blue prints, cut:
● 56—3½×6½" rectangles
**From assorted dark red, green, rust,
and purple prints, cut:**
● 352—2×6½" rectangles
From dark blue print, cut:
● 9—2½×42" binding strips
● 8—2×42" strips for inner border
From blue print, cut:
● 9—6×42" strips for outer border

Assemble the Wild Goose Chase Blocks

1. For accurate sewing lines, use a quilter's
pencil to mark a diagonal line on the wrong
side of each navy blue print 3½" square.
(To prevent your fabric from stretching as
you draw the lines, place 220-grit sandpaper
under the squares.)

2. Align a marked navy blue print 3½"
square with one end of a tan print 3½×6½"
rectangle (see Diagram 1; note the placement
of the marked diagonal line). Stitch on the
marked line; trim away the excess fabric,
leaving a ¼" seam allowance. Press the
attached triangle open.

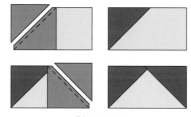

Diagram 1

3. Align a second marked navy blue print
square with the opposite end of the same
rectangle (see Diagram 1, again noting the
placement of the marked diagonal line).
Stitch on the marked line; trim and press as
before to make a tan Flying Geese unit. The
pieced Flying Geese unit should still measure
3½×6½", including the seam allowances.

4. Repeat steps 2 and 3 to make a total of 56
tan Flying Geese units.

5. Using the assorted light blue print
3½×6½" rectangles and the remaining
marked navy blue print squares, repeat steps
2 and 3 to make a total of 56 blue Flying
Geese units.

6. Sew together a tan Flying Geese unit and
a blue Flying Geese unit to make a Flying
Geese segment (see Diagram 2). Repeat to
make a total of 56 Flying Geese segments.

Diagram 2

7. Referring to Diagram 3, sew together four
Flying Geese segments in pairs. Press the
seam allowances open for the least bulk. Then
join the pairs to make a Wild Goose Chase
block. Press the seam allowances open. The
pieced block should measure 12½" square,
including the seam allowances.

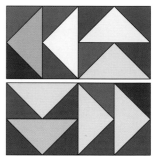

Diagram 3

8. Repeat Step 7 to make a total of 13 Wild
Goose Chase blocks. The remaining Flying
Geese segments will be used to complete the
quilt center.

Assemble the Rail Fence Blocks

1. Aligning long edges, sew together four
assorted dark red, green, rust, and purple
print 2×6½" rectangles to make a Rail
Fence unit (see Diagram 4). Press the seam
allowances in one direction. The pieced Rail
Fence unit should measure 6½" square,
including the seam allowances. Repeat to
make a total of 88 Rail Fence units.

Diagram 4

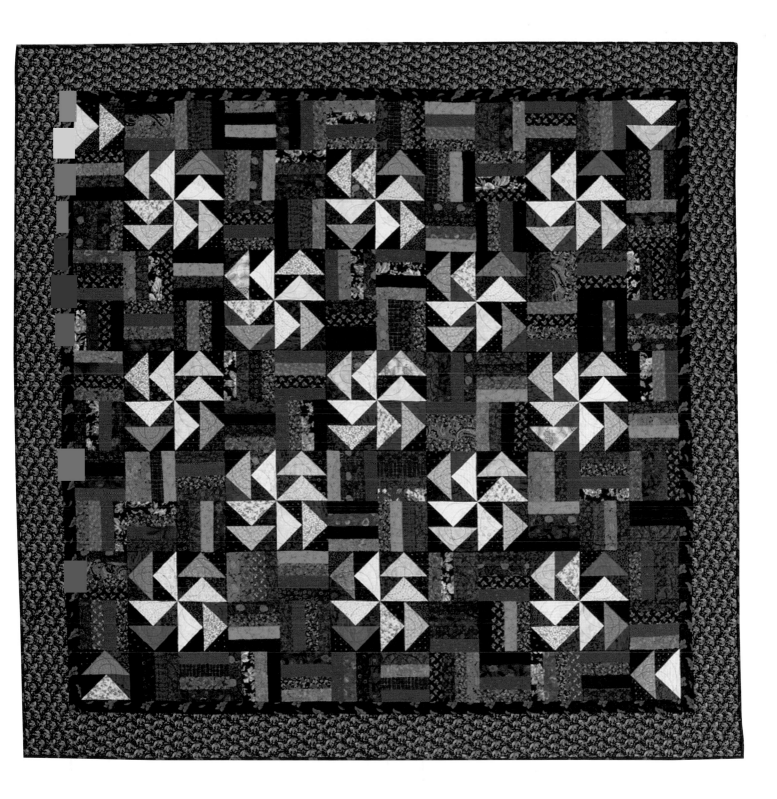

2. Lay out four Rail Fence units, paying attention to the direction of the stripes (see Diagram 5). Sew together the Rail Fence units in pairs. Press the seam allowances in opposite directions. Join the pairs to make a Rail Fence block. Press the seam allowance in one direction. The pieced block should measure 12½" square, including the seam allowances.

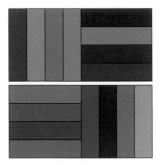

Diagram 5

3. Repeat Step 2 to make a total of 12 Rail Fence blocks. The remaining Rail Fence units will be used to complete the quilt center.

Assemble the Quilt Center

1. Referring to the Quilt Assembly Diagram, lay out the 13 Wild Goose Chase blocks, 12 Rail Fence blocks, and 20 of the remaining Rail Fence units in seven horizontal rows. Sew together the pieces in each row. Press the seam allowances open for the least bulk. Then join the rows.

2. Lay out the 20 remaining Rail Fence units and the four remaining Flying Geese

segments in two vertical rows. Sew together the units in each row. Press seam allowances open. Join the vertical rows to the pieced horizontal rows to make the quilt center. The pieced quilt center should measure 72½" square, including the seam allowances.

Add the Borders

1. Cut and piece the dark blue print 2×42" strips to make the following:
- 2—2×75½" inner border strips
- 2—2×72½" inner border strips

2. Sew the short inner border strips to opposite edges of the pieced quilt center. Then add the long inner border strips to the

Quilt Assembly Diagram

remaining edges of the quilt center. Press all seam allowances toward the border. The pieced quilt center should now measure 75½" square, including the seam allowances.

3. Cut and piece the blue print 6×42" strips to make the following:
- 2—6×86½" outer border strips
- 2—6×75½" outer border strips

4. Sew the short outer border strips to opposite edges of the pieced quilt center. Then add the long outer border strips to the remaining edges of the quilt center to complete the quilt top. Press all seam allowances toward the outer border.

Complete the Quilt

1. Cut and piece the backing fabric to measure at least 3" bigger than the quilt top on all sides. Press all seam allowances open. With wrong sides together, layer the quilt top and backing fabric with the batting in between. Baste the layers.

2. Quilt as desired. For the quilt shown, a spinning medallion was quilted in each of the blocks, alternating dark red and blue thread. A feather garland fills the borders.

3. Use the dark blue print 2½×42" strips to bind the quilt as follows.

4. Join the strips with diagonal seams to make one continuous binding strip (see Diagram 6). Trim the excess fabric, leaving ¼" seam allowances. Press the seam allowances open. Then, with the wrong sides together, fold under 1" at one end of the binding strip (see Diagram 7); press. Fold the strip in half lengthwise (see Diagram 8); press.

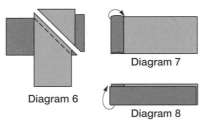

Diagram 6

Diagram 7

Diagram 8

5. Beginning in the center of one side, place the binding strip against the right side of the quilt top, aligning the binding strip's raw edges with the quilt top's raw edge (see Diagram 9). Sew through all layers, stopping ¼" from the corner. Backstitch, then clip the threads. Remove the quilt from under the sewing-machine presser foot.

Diagram 9

6. Fold the binding strip upward (see Diagram 10), creating a diagonal fold, and finger-press.

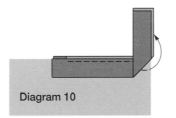

Diagram 10

7. Holding the diagonal fold in place with your finger, bring the binding strip down in line with the next edge, making a horizontal fold that aligns with the top edge of the quilt (see Diagram 11).

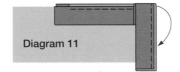

Diagram 11

8. Start sewing again at the top of the horizontal fold, stitching through all layers. Sew around the quilt, turning each corner in the same manner. When you return to the starting point, lap the binding strip inside the beginning fold (see Diagram 12). Finish sewing to the starting point (see Diagram 13). Trim the batting and backing fabric even with the quilt top's edges.

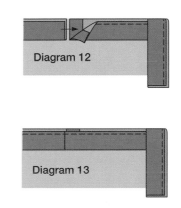

Diagram 12

Diagram 13

9. Turn the binding over the edge of the quilt to the back. Hand-stitch the binding to the backing fabric, making sure to cover any machine stitching.

10. To make mitered corners on the back, hand-stitch the binding up to a corner; fold a miter in the binding. Take a stitch or two in the fold to secure it. Then stitch the binding in place up to the next corner. Finish each corner in the same manner.

Better Homes and Gardens® Creative Collection™

Editorial Director
Gayle Goodson Butler

Editor in Chief Deborah Gore Ohrn

Executive Editor Karman Wittry Hotchkiss

Managing Editor Kathleen Armentrout

Contributing Editorial Manager Heidi Palkovic

Contributing Design Director Tracy DeVenney

Contributing Editor Laura Holtorf Collins
Copy Chief Mary Heaton
Contributing Copy Editor Mary Helen Schiltz
Proofreader Joleen F. Ross
Administrative Assistant Lori Eggers

Executive Vice President
Bob Mate

Publishing Group President
Jack Griffin

Chairman and CEO William T. Kerr
President and COO Stephen M. Lacy

In Memoriam
E. T. Meredith III (1933–2003)
